The Present

The Gift That Makes You
Happy And Successful
At Work And In Life

Other Books by Spencer Johnson, M.D.

THE PRESENT
The Gift That Makes You Happy and Successful At Work and In Life
WHO MOVED MY CHEESE? An A-Mazing Way to Deal With Change
In Your Work and In Your Life
WHO MOVED MY CHEESE? FOR TEENS An A-Mazing Way For Teens
to Change & Win!
WHO MOVED MY CHEESE? FOR KIDS An A-Mazing Way For
Kids to Change & Win! (Children's Picture Book)
THE ONE MINUTE MANAGER (co-Authored with Kenneth Blanchard,
PhD.) The World's Most Popular Management Method
THE ONE MINUTE $ALES PERSON More Sales With Less Stress
YES OR NO The Guide to Better Decisions
THE ONE MINUTE MOTHER The Quickest Way For Mothers to
Help Children Like Themselves and Behave Themselves
THE ONE MINUTE FATHER The Quickest Way For Fathers to Help
Children Like Themselves and Behave Themselves
THE ONE MINUTE TEACHER (co-Authored with Constance Johnson,
M.Ed.) How to Teach Others to Teach Themselves
THE PRECIOUS PRESENT The Gift You Give Yourself
ONE MINUTE FOR YOURSELF Taking Care of Your Most Valuable Asset

THE VALUETALE® SERIES for children:
THE VALUE OF BELIEVING IN YOURSELF, The Story of Louis Pasteur
THE VALUE OF PATIENCE, The Story of the Wright Brothers
THE VALUE OF KINDNESS, The Story of Elizabeth Fry
THE VALUE OF HUMOR, The Story of Will Rogers
THE VALUE OF COURAGE, The Story of Jackie Robinson
THE VALUE OF CURIOSITY, The Story of Christopher Columbus
THE VALUE OF IMAGINATION, The Story of Charles Dickens
THE VALUE OF SAVING, The Story of Ben Franklin
THE VALUE OF SHARING, The Story of the Mayo Brothers
THE VALUE OF HONESTY, The Story of Confucius
THE VALUE OF UNDERSTANDING, The Story of Margaret Mead
THE VALUE OF FANTASY, The Story of Hans Christian Andersen
THE VALUE OF DEDICATION, The Story of Albert Schweitzer

The Present

*The Gift That Makes You
Happy And Successful
At Work And In Life*

Spencer
Johnson, M.D.

BANTAM BOOKS

LONDON • NEW YORK • TORONTO • SYDNEY • AUCKLAND

Dedicated to
all of the people who are
a part of this book,
especially my family.

THE PRESENT
A BANTAM BOOK: 0 553 81666 7

First publication in Great Britain
Originally published in the United States by Doubleday,
a division of Random House, Inc.

PRINTING HISTORY
Bantam edition published 2003

1 3 5 7 9 10 8 6 4 2

Set in 14/16.3pt Times New Roman by
Falcon Oast Graphic Art Ltd.

Bantam Books are published by Transworld Publishers,
61–63 Uxbridge Road, London W5 5SA,
a division of The Random House Group Ltd,
in Australia by Random House Australia (Pty) Ltd,
20 Alfred Street, Milsons Point, Sydney, NSW 2061, Australia,
in New Zealand by Random House New Zealand Ltd,
18 Poland Road, Glenfield, Auckland 10, New Zealand
and in South Africa by Random House (Pty) Ltd,
Endulini, 5a Jubilee Road, Parktown 2193, South Africa.

Printed and bound in Great Britain by
Mackays of Chatham, Chatham, Kent

Papers used by Transworld Publishers are natural, recyclable products
made from wood grown in sustainable forests. The manufacturing processes
conform to the environmental regulations of the country of origin.

www.THEPRESENT.com

Table of Contents

Before The Story

Late one afternoon, Bill Green received an urgent phone call from Liz Michaels, who he used to work with.

She had heard Bill was experiencing great success, and she got right to the point, "Could I meet with you soon?" she asked. He thought he heard a strain in her voice.

Bill said yes and rearranged his schedule so they could meet for lunch the next day. When Liz entered the restaurant, he noticed how tired she looked.

After some small talk and ordering their meals, Liz told him, "I have Harrison's job now."

"Congratulations," Bill said. "I'm not surprised you've been promoted."

"Thanks, but the problems are mounting," she admitted.

"A lot has changed since you were with us. We have fewer people, but more work. There never seems to be enough time to get everything done – at work or at home.

"And I'm just not enjoying life as much as I'd like to.

"By the way, Bill," she added, changing the subject, "you look good."

"I *am* good," he said. "I'm enjoying my work and life more. It's a nice change for me!"

"Oh?" she said. "Did your job change?"

Bill laughed. "No, but it feels like it. It all came together about a year ago."

"What happened?" Liz wanted to know.

Bill began, "Remember how hard I used to push myself and others to get good results? And how much time and effort it took us to get things done?"

Liz laughed. "I remember all too well."

Bill smiled, as though amused by his old behavior. "Well I've learned a few things. And so have many other people in my department. We're getting better results, faster and with less stress.

"And to top it off, I'm enjoying life more."

"What's happened?" Liz asked.

"If I told you, you probably wouldn't believe it."

"Try me," she replied.

He paused and then said, "I heard a story from a good friend of mine. It turned out to be a real gift. In fact, the story is called The Present."

"What is it about?" Liz inquired.

"It's a story about a young man who discovers a way to live and work that makes him happier and more successful.

"After I heard it, I thought a lot about the story and how I could benefit from using it. I started using what I learned, first at work and then later in my personal life. It had a big impact on me, and others began to notice.

"Like the young man in the story, I'm happier now, and I'm doing a lot better."

"How?" Liz asked. "In what way?"

"Well, I now concentrate better on what I am doing. I learn more from what happens, and I'm able to plan better. I can focus now on getting the more important things done, without taking so long to do them."

"You got all that out of one story?" Liz seemed amazed.

"Well, that's what *I* got out of the story. Different people get different things from The Present, depending on where they are in their work or life when they hear it. Of course, some people just don't get it at all.

"The story is a practical parable," Bill continued. "So it's not just what's *in* the story. It's what you take *out* of it that gives it value."

Liz asked, "Can you tell it to me?"

Bill sipped his glass of water and then said slowly, "Liz, I hesitate because you've always seemed to be so skeptical. And this is the type of story you might dismiss too easily."

At that point, Liz let her guard down. She confessed that she was under a great deal of stress, in her job and personal life, and had come to lunch hoping to get some help.

Bill remembered when he felt that way.

Liz said, "I really want to hear the story."

Bill had always liked and respected Liz. So he said, "I'd be happy to tell it to you, if you agree that what you get and use from the story is up to you.

"And," he added, "if you find it useful, that you will share it with others."

Liz agreed and Bill continued. "When I first heard it, I realized at some point in the story that there was a great deal more to it than I had anticipated.

"I found myself taking notes throughout the story to help me remember the insights I might want to use later."

Liz wondered what she might find useful for herself. She took out a small notepad and said, "I'm ready to listen."

Then Bill began to tell the story of The Present.

The Story
Of
The Present

ONCE there was a boy, who listened to a wise old man, and thus began to learn about The Present.

The old man and the boy had known each other for more than a year, and enjoyed talking together.

One day the old man said, "It is called simply 'The Present' because, of all the gifts you might receive, you will find this present is *the* most valuable one of all."

"Why is it so valuable?" the boy asked.

The old man explained. "Because when you receive this gift, you become happier and better able to do whatever you want to do."

"Wow!" the little boy exclaimed, although not fully understanding. "I hope someone gives me The Present someday. Maybe I'll get it for my birthday."

Then the boy ran off to play.

The old man smiled.

He wondered how many birthdays would pass before the boy would realize the value of The Present.

The old man enjoyed watching the boy play in the neighborhood.

He often saw a smile on the youngster's face and heard him laughing as he swung from a nearby tree.

The boy was happy and completely engaged in whatever he was doing. He was a joy to behold.

As the boy grew older, the old man couldn't help but notice the way the boy worked.

On Saturday mornings, he would occasionally observe his young friend mowing the lawn across the street.

The boy actually whistled while he worked. He seemed to be happy no matter what he was doing.

One morning the boy saw the old man, and remembered what the old man had told him about The Present.

The boy knew all about presents, like the bicycle he got for his last birthday and the gifts he'd found under the tree on Christmas morning.

But as he thought more about it, he realized that the joy of those presents didn't last very long.

He wondered, "What is so special about The Present?

"What could make it so much better than any other present?

"What could make me happier, and better at doing things?"

Wanting answers to his questions, he crossed the street to ask the old man.

He asked what a young boy might ask. "Is The Present like a magic wand that can make all my wishes come true?"

"No," the old man answered with a laugh. "The Present is not about magic or wishing."

Unsure of the old man's answer, the boy returned to his work mowing the lawn, still wondering about The Present.

As he grew older, the boy continued to wonder about The Present. If it has nothing to do with wishing, could it have something to do with going away to someplace special?

Did it mean traveling to a foreign land, where everything looked different: the people, the clothes they wore, the language they spoke, the houses they lived in, even their money? How would he get there?

He went to see the old man.

"Is The Present," he asked, "a time machine that I could get in and go anywhere I wanted?"

"No," the old man replied. "When you receive The Present, you no longer spend your time dreaming about being somewhere else."

TIME passed and the boy grew into his teens.

He became more and more dissatisfied. He had hoped he would be happier as he grew older. But he always seemed to want more – more friends, more things, more excitement.

In his impatience, he dreamed about what awaited him out in the world. His thoughts drifted back to his talks with the old man and he found himself thinking more and more about the promise of The Present.

He approached the old man again and asked, "Is The Present something that will make me rich?"

"Yes, in a way it can," the old man told him. "The Present can lead you to many kinds of riches. But its value is not measured in gold or money alone."

The teenager was confused.

"You told me that when you receive The Present, you are happier."

"Yes," the old man said. "And better able to do whatever you set out to do. In other words – to be successful."

"What do you mean by successful?" the teenager asked.

"Success is progressing toward whatever you think is important," the old man answered. "For you, it may be getting good grades in school, doing well in sports, having a good relationship with your parents, getting a good part time job after school, and then getting a raise because you do the job so well – or just enjoying life and appreciating what you have."

"So, I get to decide what success is for myself?" the teenager asked.

"We all do," the old man said. "Success is something we all define for ourselves at different stages of our lives."

"Well, no one has ever given me a gift like that. In fact, I've never heard anyone else talk about such a present. I am beginning to think it doesn't exist."

The old man replied, "Oh, it exists. But I'm afraid you don't yet understand."

*You Already Know
What The Present Is.*

*You Already Know
Where To Find It.*

*And You Already Know
How It Can Make You
Happy And Successful.*

*You Knew It Best When
You Were Younger.*

You Have Simply Forgotten.

The old man inquired, "When you were younger, mowing the lawn, was that a good time or a bad time for you?"

"A good time," the once-little-boy answered.

"What made it good?" the old man asked.

The teenager thought for a moment, and said, "Because I loved what I was doing. I did such a good job that our neighbors asked me to cut their lawns as well. In fact I made quite a lot of money for a kid my age."

"And what did you think about as you worked?" the old man inquired.

"When I was mowing the lawn, I thought about mowing the lawn. I thought about how I'd mowed the grass through the tricky areas and around the obstacles. I thought about how many lawns I was able to finish in an afternoon, and how I could work so well. But mostly I just concentrated on cutting the grass in front of me."

He spoke about mowing the grass in a tone that made it sound like the answer should be obvious.

The old man leaned forward and said, "Exactly. And that is why you were so happy and successful."

Unfortunately, the teenager did not take the time to reflect on what he had just heard. Instead, he became more impatient.

"If you really want me to be happy," the teenager said, "why don't you just tell me what The Present is?"

"And where to find it?" the old man volleyed back.

"Yes, exactly," the teen demanded.

"I would like to," the old man responded, "but I do not have such power. No one can find The Present for someone else.

"The Present is a gift you give to yourself. Only *you* have the power to discover what it is," the old man explained.

The teen was disappointed with the answer and left the old man.

As the teen grew into a young man, he resolved to find The Present on his own.

He read magazines, newspapers and books. He talked with his friends and family. He scoured the Internet. He even traveled far and wide seeking answers from everyone he met. But no matter how hard he searched, he could not find anyone who was able to tell him what The Present was.

After a while, he became so tired and discouraged that he simply gave up his search.

Eventually, the young man took a job working for a local company. To those around him he seemed to be doing well enough. But he felt that something was missing.

When he was at work, he thought about where else he might enjoy working more. Or he thought about what he would do when he got home.

His mind often wandered at meetings and even in conversations with his friends. During meals, he was often distracted and unaware of the taste of his food.

In his job, he dealt adequately with his projects, but he knew he could do better. He knew in his heart he was not giving it all he could, but he didn't feel what he did really mattered.

AFTER a while the young man realized he had become unhappy. He thought he worked hard and that he did what he was expected to do. He usually arrived on time and felt he put in a full day's work.

He had hoped to be promoted. Perhaps that would make him happy.

Then one day he learned he had been passed over for the promotion he thought he was entitled to.

The young man became angry. He didn't understand why he had been passed over for the promotion. He tried his best not to let his anger show as it was not welcomed at work. However, he could not let his anger go and it began to consume him.

As the young man's anger increased, the quality of his work decreased.

To those around him, he tried to act like the promotion didn't matter. But deep down inside he began to doubt himself, "Do I have what it takes to succeed?" he wondered.

The young man's personal life wasn't much better. He hadn't been able to get over breaking up with his girlfriend. He worried over whether he would ever find true love and have a family of his own.

He found himself floundering. His life seemed to be a series of loose ends, unfinished projects, and unattained goals and dreams.

He knew that he was not fulfilling the promise he'd showed when he was younger.

Every day the young man came home from work a little more tired and disappointed. He never seemed satisfied with what he was doing. But he did not know what to do.

He thought about his youth, and recalled the days when life seemed simpler. He thought about the words of the old man, and the promise of The Present.

He knew he was not as happy, or as successful, as he wanted to be.

Perhaps he should not have abandoned his search for The Present.

It had been a long time since he had spoken to the old man. He was embarrassed about how badly things were going for him, and was reluctant to go back and ask for help.

Finally, however, he was so dissatisfied with his work and life, that he knew he had to talk to the old man.

THE old man was pleased to see him. He immediately noticed the young man's lack of energy and obvious unhappiness. Concerned, he encouraged the young man to tell him what was on his mind.

The young man described his earlier frustrating attempts to find The Present and how he had given up his search for it. He talked about his current troubles.

But, to the young man's surprise, things didn't seem so bad in the old man's presence.

The young man and the old man had a wonderful time together talking and laughing.

The young man realized how much he liked to be with the old man. He felt happier and more energetic in his presence.

He wondered why the old man seemed more alive than most other people he knew. What was it that made him so special?

He said to the old man, "I feel so good when I am with you. Does it have something to do with The Present?"

"It has *everything* to do with it," the old man answered.

The young man said, "I wish I could find The Present."

The old man gazed kindly on the young man and told him, "In order to find The Present for yourself, think of the times when you were the happiest, and most successful.

"You know where to find The Present already. You are just not aware of it."

He continued, "When you stop trying so hard, you will find it is easier to discover. In fact, it will become obvious."

Then the old man suggested, "Why don't you take some time away from your regular routine and let the answer come to you."

FOLLOWING the old man's suggestion, the young man accepted a friend's offer to spend some time at his cabin in the mountains.

Alone in the woods, the young man found things moved at a slower pace and life looked different.

He took long walks and reflected on his life. "Why isn't my life like the old man's?" he wondered.

The young man had learned that while the old man was modest, he had been very successful in the world.

He had started at the bottom of a highly respected organization and had risen to the very top. He had helped the community in many ways.

The old man had a strong and loving family and many loyal friends who often came to see him. He had a wonderful sense of humor, and a wisdom others enjoyed and respected.

Most of all, there was a calm about him that the young man had rarely encountered.

The young man smiled. "And he has the youthful energy of someone half his age."

The old man was clearly the happiest and most successful person he had ever met.

So, what was The Present that gave the old man so many good qualities?

As the young man walked for miles around the lake, he reflected on what he knew about The Present: *It was a gift that you give to yourself. He'd known it best when he was younger. He'd simply forgotten it.*

However, his mind drifted back to his failures. He remembered exactly where he was when he found out he didn't get the coveted promotion. It was as if it had happened yesterday. He was still angry.

The more he thought about it, the more he worried about going back to work.

Then he noticed it was growing dark and he hurried back to the cabin.

Once inside, he lit a fire to ward off the chill. He noticed something he hadn't seen before.

As he stared at the fire, he became aware of the cabin's great fireplace for the first time.

It was made of large and small stones. A minimum of mortar held one stone to the next. Someone had very carefully chosen, chiseled and perfectly placed each stone.

Now that he was aware of it, he appreciated and enjoyed what had been right in front of him all along.

Whoever had built the fireplace was more than a mason. He was an artist.

As the young man marveled at how extraordinarily well built the fireplace was, he thought about how the mason must have felt as he worked.

He must have been completely focused on the job before him. It was clear the mason's thoughts had not wandered or strayed very often. The work was that good.

It was unlikely that he had been thinking about a past love or that night's dinner. Nor could his thoughts have raced on to what he would do when he was finished. Or what he could have been doing that he might have enjoyed more.

The young man could tell by looking at the marvelous masonry that he must have concentrated on nothing else but the task at hand.

The mason had obviously succeeded.

What was it the old man had said? "To find The Present, think of the times when you were happiest, and most successful."

The young man recalled talking with the old man about mowing lawns when he was a boy. He remembered how he had focused on cutting the grass and had not let anything else distract him.

"When you are fully engaged in what you are doing your mind doesn't wander and you are happy," the old man had said. *"You are intent only on what is happening at that moment."*

He realized he had not felt that way for a long time – about work or anything else. He spent too much time being upset about the past or worried about the future.

The young man gazed at the inside of the cabin. He stared again into the fire. At that moment, he wasn't thinking about the past. And he wasn't anxious about what might happen in the future.

He simply appreciated where he was, and what he was doing.

Then he smiled. He realized he felt good.

He was simply enjoying what he was doing. He enjoyed being in the present moment.

In a rush, it hit him. Of course!

He knew what The Present was ... what it had always been:

*The Present
Is Not The Past And
It Is Not The Future.*

*The Present Is
The Present Moment!*

*The Present Is
Now!*

The young man broke into a smile. It was so obvious! He took in a deep breath and relaxed. He looked around the cabin and appreciated it in a whole new way.

He went outside and saw the silhouette of the trees against the night sky and the snow atop the distant mountains.

He saw the moon's early reflection on the lake and heard the birds' late evening song.

He was now aware of so many things that had been right in front of him all along, but he had not seen or felt them before.

Now he felt more peaceful and happy than he had felt in a long time. He didn't feel like a failure. The more the young man thought about The Present, the more sense it made.

Being in The Present means focusing on what is happening right now! It means appreciating the gifts you are offered every day.

It occurred to him that whenever he was in The Present, he was more aware and focused on whatever he was doing. He was more like the masonry artist who had built the great stone fireplace.

Now he realized what the old man had been trying to tell him since he was a boy.

When you are in The Present, you feel happy and successful.

The next morning, the young man awoke refreshed. He could hardly wait to go and tell the old man what he had discovered.

As he dressed for the day, he was amazed at how much more energy he had.

He remembered how he had been the night before. He made his discovery when he focused on where he was, and what he was doing, right *then* and *there*. He was thinking about nothing else.

He was glad he had come to the mountains to think. And it had helped to be on his own.

He reminded himself to be in The Present right now. He took in a deep breath, and regained a sense of peace about him.

He thought, *It is amazing how simple it is, and how fast it works.*

Then he frowned and asked himself, "Could The Present really be that simple? After all, isn't life complicated? Things certainly seem complicated at work.

"Could simply being in The Present make you feel happy and successful?" He had to admit it seemed to be working for him.

But, as he prepared to leave, he began to wonder.

How does The Present work when the situation you are in is not as enjoyable as being in a great mountain cabin? It is one thing to be in a good situation but quite another to be in a bad one.

And what, if anything, is the importance of The Past or The Future?

As he journeyed toward the old man, he realized he had many questions he wanted to ask him.

Being

THE moment the old man saw the young man approaching with a wide smile and clear look in his eyes, the old man called out, "You look like someone who has found The Present!"

"I have!" the young man exclaimed.

The old man beamed. He knew the young man would find his way. They both enjoyed the moment.

Then the old man said, "Tell me how it happened."

"Well, I found myself feeling happy and realized that I wasn't thinking about what had happened to me in The Past, and I wasn't feeling anxious about what might happen in The Future.

"All of a sudden, the obvious occurred to me. The Present, the gift you give yourself, is just that – the present moment. I see now that being in The Present means focusing on what *is,* right now."

The old man said, "That is true in two ways."

The young man was not listening. He continued talking. "I was in a good situation when I found The Present. I was in my friend's mountain cabin."

Then he asked hesitantly, "I was wondering how does being in The Present help when you are in a bad situation?"

The old man responded with a question. "When you became aware of The Present were you thinking about what was right or wrong at that time?"

"I was thinking about what was right. I knew I was in a beautiful place and I was enjoying the quiet time."

The old man said, "Consider this:

Even In The Most
Difficult Situations,

When You Focus On
What Is <u>Right</u>
In The Present Moment,
It Makes You Happier,

And Gives You The Needed
Energy And Confidence
To Deal With
What Is Wrong.

What the old man said surprised the young man. "So being in The Present means focusing on what *is,* right now.

"And, it also means focusing on what is *right*, now."

"Yes," the old man said.

The young man thought more about it. "You know that makes sense. When I'm in a bad situation, I usually focus on what's wrong and that gets me down and discouraged."

The old man said. "Many people do that. In reality, most situations are a mix of good and bad, right and wrong. It depends on how you look at them.

"The more you look at what is wrong," the old man said, "the less energy and confidence you have. That's why, when you find yourself in a 'bad' situation, it's important to look for what is *right*, even if it is hard to find. Then appreciate it and build on it.

"The more you appreciate what is right at the moment, the happier you are. You become more relaxed, and it is easier then to stay in The Present."

The young man asked, "What if The Present is very painful, like experiencing the loss of a loved one?"

"Pain," the old man offered, "is the difference between what is, and what you want it to be.

"Pain in The Present, like everything else, is constantly changing. It will come and go.

"When you stay fully in The Present and have felt the pain, and feel drained by it, you can begin to look for what is right, and build on it."

The young man began to write notes to help him remember what he was discovering.

He said, "Why do I get the feeling that what I have learned so far is just the tip of the iceberg, and that there is a lot more beneath the surface?"

The old man said, "Because you have just begun to appreciate what is waiting out there for you to discover."

He offered, "Since you have found The Present on your own, and seem keen to know more, I am happy to share what I know with you."

The young man said he would appreciate it, so the old man continued.

"It is important to experience painful situations and learn from them," he said, "rather than try to distract yourself with something else."

Being In The Present Means
Tuning Out Distractions

And Paying Attention To
What Is Important, Now.

You Create Your Own Present
By What You Give
Your Attention To.

The young man said, "So, even in difficult situations, I need to tune out the unimportant distractions that keep me from being in The Present."

"You can take examples from your own life," the old man said. "You said earlier that you were having difficulties at work, and in your old relationship.

"You might want to ask yourself, 'Was I often distracted at work or did I usually pay full attention to what was important then?'

"Think about your life outside of work.

"How present were you when you were with your sweetheart? Was she important enough for you to focus your wholehearted attention on her when you were together?

"In a relationship, you need to focus on the whole person. By being more aware of their 'good' and 'bad' qualities, you can address potential problems, instead of being side-tracked by them.

"Rather than provide you with examples of how other people use The Present to be happy and successful, it will prove more meaningful for you to discover them for yourself in the coming weeks."

The young man said, "Before I go, can I ask you about The Past and The Future?"

The old man responded, "We'll get to those important areas later. For now, let's stay with The Present.

"As you stay in The Present and focus only on what is important right now, you will make many wonderful discoveries of your own."

Before he left, the young man wrote down a summary of what he had discovered so far about being in The Present:

Focus on what is happening at the moment.

Appreciate what is right about the situation, and build on it.

Pay attention to what is important now.

He thanked the old man and said he was ready to go to work and try to apply what he had discovered.

He knew this meant being aware of both the good and bad in a present situation, so he could overcome obstacles that might keep him from being successful.

THE next week at work, the young man reviewed the notes he had taken during his conversations with the old man.

Then he sat down to finish a project that had been hanging over his head for a while. He'd been putting it off because he believed it would be difficult to gather all the necessary information.

Then he remembered to use what he had learned.

He took a moment to be in The Present. He took in a deep breath, looked around him, and appreciated what was *right* now!

He realized he may not have been promoted, but he still had his job. He had a good working environment that was fairly quiet and well organized.

And he still had plenty of opportunity to do his job in a way that would earn him recognition.

He realized it was all too easy to forget to enjoy what he had right now.

Then he focused on what was important now. He knew he needed to make progress on one project and use that to build his energy and confidence to succeed in the next task.

He began working through the problems one by one. He ran into a couple of stumbling blocks. However, instead of becoming distracted and working on something else, he stayed in The Present.

He focused solely on what he needed to do at the moment and kept going.

To his amazement, he was finished in a couple of hours. Even though it was a small project, he felt good about the work, knowing he had done a thorough job.

He thought, "It's been a long time since I've felt this good at work.

"Staying in The Present is really working for me."

The young man proceeded to immerse himself in his job in the weeks that followed, displaying the kind of intensity and focus those around him had rarely seen.

Before he had learned about The Present, he used to daydream during meetings, thinking about the promotion he hoped would happen.

Now, he knew it was important to be present if he was going to do a good job.

When others spoke up, he let go of what he had been thinking about, and focused on what they were saying. He made a concerted effort to join in, challenging himself to offer at least one new idea.

Soon his customers and others at work noticed the change in the young man. His old distracted manner changed into a genuine interest in their needs, and in what he could do to help them and the organization.

In his personal life, his friends noticed the change too. He listened more carefully to what they said, in the same way the old man had listened to him.

At first, he had to work hard to focus on The Present, and not drift into regret about The Past or worry about The Future. But as he practiced being in The Present, he found it became easier.

As a result of his changed outlook, his work and life improved.

His increased passion and commitment caught the attention of his boss, as well as his friends.

He was beginning to realize that he was more likely to get promoted when he worked better, and really deserved to be rewarded. His resentment toward his boss began to fade, at least at times.

Perhaps, most important, he had met a wonderful young woman and was developing a great relationship with her.

Everything seemed to be going better for him. The young man felt more alive and in control of his life. He felt more confident, stronger and more productive.

He was appreciative of what he had, was paying attention to what was important, and most of all he was *enjoying* it.

No wonder the old man said The Present is the best gift you can give yourself.

However, just when he thought he knew how to be in The Present, a problem arose.

The difficulty began when he was working with someone else on a project for his boss. The other person made little effort, and offered few ideas. Rather than talking to the person about pulling their weight, or telling his boss about the problem, the young man took on the work himself.

Before long, he had fallen behind.

Then he missed a deadline.

It was an important project and his boss expressed his disappointment.

The young man thought he had failed. His confidence in his newfound abilities began to slip away.

What had gone wrong? He thought he had been fully absorbed in the present moment.

The disappointed young man sat with his shoulders slumped and his head looking down at his desk. He felt tired.

He wondered what the old man would do in the same situation.

Uncertain, he returned to talk with the old man.

Learning

THE old man greeted him warmly. "I've been expecting you."

The young man began, "You told me that being in The Present would make me happy and successful at what I do.

"I work hard at staying in The Present, and I can already see the good it has done me. But it seems as if it's not enough."

"I'm not surprised," the old man said. "To fully embrace The Present you must do more than just live in the present moment.

"But I waited for you to discover this for yourself."

The old man asked the young man to tell him about the problem and then said, "So, you reacted to the other person's lack of support by shouldering the burden, rather than addressing the problem."

Then he asked, "Haven't you told me that you've done this same sort of thing before?"

"Yes," the young man admitted. "It's because I've always disliked confrontation. My boss told me it's one of the reasons I have trouble with managing and leading."

Then he added, "And it's not just at work. My old girlfriend said I ignored our problems, too. It's one of the reasons we broke up.

"And, every now and then I think about the promotion I didn't get. I don't know why I am having such a hard time letting go of that."

The old man said, "Perhaps this will help:

*It Is Hard To
Let Go Of The Past
If You Have Not Learned
From The Past.*

*As Soon As You
Learn And Let Go
You Improve The Present.*

"I like that," the young man said. "It makes a lot of sense."

Then he asked, "Do you mind if I change the subject and ask you how you know so much?"

The old man laughed and said, "Well, I spent many years working for an interesting organization. I listened to what people were saying about their work and lives. Some were having a difficult time, while others were doing well. But I noticed there were common patterns."

The young man asked, "What did you notice about the people who were having a difficult time?"

The old man could sense what the young man was going through. "It is interesting to see that you did not ask first about the people who were doing well."

"Ouch," the young man said.

" 'Ouch' is right. You may want to look at why you do that." Then the old man said, "I know you are having difficulties, so let's start there if you like.

"Many of the people who had the most difficulties were worried about the mistakes they had made, or about the mistakes they were afraid they might make," the old man said. "Some were angry about something that had happened to them at work in The Past."

"I know that feeling," replied the young man.

"The ones who were doing well concentrated on their work at that moment. They made mistakes like everybody else, but they were able to learn from them, let go, and move on. And they did not talk as much about what was wrong."

The old man continued, "It seems to me, rather than look at your Past and learn from it, you choose to ignore it.

"Many people avoid looking at The Past, because they do not want to be troubled by it. They say things like, 'My past experiences brought me to where I am today.' They don't ask themselves where they would be today if they had looked at their past experiences, and learned from the things that didn't go well.

"As a result, they learn nothing."

The young man said, "So, like me, they keep making the same mistakes. In those areas, their Present is just like their Past."

"Well said," the old man responded. "When you do not use your feelings about The Past to learn from your experiences, you lose the joy of The Present. Once you have truly learned from The Past, it is easier to enjoy The Present.

"While it is true that one must not live in The Past – for then you are *not* living in The Present – it is important to *use* The Past to learn from your mistakes. Or, if you've done well in The Past, look at why and build on your successes."

The young man was confused. He asked, "When should I be in The Present, and when should I learn from The Past?"

"That's a good question," replied the old man.

You might find this useful:

Anytime You Are
Unhappy In The Present
Or Feeling Unsuccessful,

It Is Time To
Learn From The Past
Or Plan For The Future.

"Only two things can rob you of the joy of The Present: your negative thoughts about The Past, or your negative thoughts about The Future."

The old man offered, "You may find it most helpful to begin by looking first at what you think about The Past.

"We'll get to The Future later," the old man promised.

The young man said, "So, anytime I feel something is interfering with my enjoying The Present and doing well, that is the time to look at The Past and learn from it."

"Yes," the old man replied.

"The time to learn," he confirmed, "is anytime you want to make The Present better than The Past.

"When you feel upset, or have any other negative feelings about The Past that are interfering with The Present, that is when you need to take the time to look at the Past and learn from it."

The young man asked, "Why is it a good time to learn when I am feeling something negative?"

The old man answered, "Because you can use your feelings to teach you."

"So how do I learn?"

The old man answered, "The best way I know of is to ask yourself three questions and answer them as honestly and realistically as you can:

"What happened in the past?

"What did I learn from it?

"What can I do differently now?"

The young man said, "In other words you think about a mistake you made, and see how you could do it differently now."

"Yes. And don't be too hard on yourself. Remember that you did the best you knew how at the time. When you know better now, you can do better now."

The young man said, "So, when you behave in the same way, you get the same results. But, when you behave differently, you get different results."

The old man said, "Yes, the good news is the more you learn from The Past, the fewer regrets you have. And the more time you have in The Present."

Before he left, the young man made several more notes:

*Look At What Happened
In The Past.*

*Learn Something
Valuable From It.*

*Use What You Learn
To Improve The Present.*

You Cannot Change The Past,
But You Can Learn From It.

When The Same Situation Arises,
You Can Do Things Differently
And Enjoy
A More Successful Present.

ON his way to work the next morning the young man thought about what the old man had said.

That day, he worked hard at staying fully engaged in the present moment, and he looked for opportunities to learn from The Past.

When the same person once again failed to contribute her part of the task, he talked with her about his concerns.

At first she seemed to resent and resist the young man's requests. But when they completed their meeting, she was happy that the young man had been honest with her. She understood the need to get the job done right. She even said she looked forward to it.

The young man felt good that he had learned from his past experience, and had acted differently. In the weeks ahead, drawing on what he had learned, the young man became more effective at his job.

His relationship with others at work improved, too. As a result his boss gave him more responsibility, and he was promoted.

In his personal life, his relationship with the young woman he was spending more and more time with continued to grow into something that was very important to both of them.

For a time, he thrived.

However, as he faced the increasing demands on his time that his new position demanded, he found it difficult to juggle everything successfully.

Still, he was often able to take a deep breath and focus on the present moment, and that helped a good deal.

Yet, he arrived each morning with more and more work to do.

He had not developed a daily schedule and was not certain what to work on first. Turning from this project to that, he spent too much time on things that were not important, while important tasks that needed to move along went unattended.

Before long, projects spun out of his control. When his boss confronted him, the young man could only throw up his hands at the amount of work he had, with too little time to do it. His boss began to wonder if he should have promoted the young man.

Discouraged and uncertain about what to do, the young man once again went to visit his friend the old man.

Planning

"**How** are you?" the old man asked.

The young man laughed uneasily and said, "Sometimes good, other times not so good." Then he talked about his difficulties.

"I don't understand," the young man said. "I've been fully immersed in The Present.

"People comment about my ability to focus so intently on what I am doing.

"I have worked at drawing from The Past, without dwelling on past regrets. I use what I've learned and I do better now.

"Yet I can't handle everything. Maybe the job is just too big for me."

The old man nodded. "At the moment, it may be. What you don't realize is that there is one last element of The Present you haven't discovered yet.

"Yes, you are learning from The Past, and using these lessons to improve The Present. And by living fully in The Present, I sense you are more appreciative of the world around you and more effective in it. So, you are making great progress.

"However, what you haven't grasped yet is the importance of the third element – The Future."

The young man said, "But when I live too much in The Future, I feel anxious. I know that when I daydream about the house I want to own, or the promotions I hope to receive, or the family I want to have, I'm not living in The Present. And I feel lost."

The old man said, "While it is not wise to *be* in The Future, for that is how you lose yourself in worry or anxiety, it is important to *plan* for The Future.

"The only way to make The Future better than The Present, other than to get lucky, is to plan for it.

"And, even if you happen to get 'lucky,' your luck can run out. And that can lead to deeper problems and a whole new set of issues to deal with. So you can't depend on getting lucky.

"Planning for The Future reduces fear and uncertainty, because you are actively taking steps toward future success. You know what you are doing and why you are doing it."

The young man wanted to know, "How does planning for The Future relate to being in The Present?"

The old man replied, "Once you have prepared for The Future, you can enjoy The Present with less anxiety.

"Planning takes much of the guesswork out of what you need to do each day. You have a road map. It lets you focus on what you need to do in The Present to help bring about The Future you want."

The young man said, "So, by planning for The Future, you can more fully be in The Present."

"Yes. You may want to think of it this way:

No One Can Predict
Or Control The Future.

However, The More You Plan
For What You Want To See Happen,

The Less Anxious You Are
In The Present,

And The More The Future
Is Known To You.

The old man continued, "A lack of planning, both at work and in our lives, is the most common reason we fall short of our dreams and our goals."

The young man asked, "So, when do I plan for The Future?"

The old man said, "Anytime you want to make The Future better than The Present."

The young man asked, "And what have you found is the best way to do that?"

The old man offered, "By thinking about these three things:

"What would a wonderful future be like?

"What are my plans to make it happen?

"What am I doing today to make it happen?

"The more you can paint a realistic picture of what you would like your future to look like, and believe it is possible to achieve, the easier it is for you to create your plan.

"And once you have a plan, you need to continually revise it as you gather more information and experience, so that the plan becomes more realistic.

"The important thing is to *do* something every day, even if you think it is a small thing, to help make that wonderful future happen."

The young man wrote:

*Picture What A Wonderful Future
Would Be Like.*

*Create A Realistic Plan
To Help It Happen.*

*Put Your Plan Into Action
In The Present.*

A light shone in the young man's eyes. "You know that's true. When I don't plan and set goals at work, or anticipate future problems, I lose my way.

"I'm more likely to spend time on things that don't matter, and leave less time for the things that really need my attention.

"I'm beginning to see now that's why I'm feeling so overwhelmed. I don't take the time to plan first and then work my plan."

The old man suggested, "You may want to think of the three parts of The Present as a tripod supporting a valuable camera, perfectly balanced by its three supporting legs: Living in The Present; Learning from The Past; and Planning for The Future.

"Remove one leg and the tripod topples over. But supported by all three, it works. And so will your life.

"However, if you are not in The Present, you will not be aware of what is going on. If you have not learned from The Past, you are not ready to plan for The Future. And if you have no plan for The Future, you are adrift.

"When you balance your work and life on a tripod of The Present, The Past and The Future – you get a much clearer picture.

"And you can deal better with whatever comes along."

REFLECTING on what the old man had told him, the young man returned to work more excited and with more clarity.

Each morning, he planned his day in advance, knowing it would help him meet his goals, while remaining flexible enough to handle the day's surprises. He set goals for each week, and each month in the same way.

Well before meetings, he reviewed what he wanted to accomplish.

When informed of a deadline, he set up a schedule, with a time for specific tasks.

He found himself using the same kind of planning in his personal life, as well. He entered events on his calendar and planned accordingly.

When meeting friends, he left extra time to get there. At home and at work he stopped waiting until the last moment.

By planning for The Future, and using it to enhance The Present, he was better able to motivate others and accomplish more. And he had never felt happier, and more in command of his life.

Over time, his boss, recognizing how productive he was, promoted him again.

And perhaps most important, the young man had become engaged and had joined his life partner in planning their future together.

The young man now went to work each day, using what he had learned to stay in The Present, learn from The Past, and plan for The Future.

It was paying off. He was good at his job, had the respect of those he worked with, and was confident he could handle most tasks.

Then, one day, the young man attended a budget meeting. He knew the company's sales of their current products were falling. The economy had slowed, but he had to admit that some of the competitors were offering better products at lower costs.

So, he was not surprised when the financial people recommended an across-the-board cut in costs. That meant that he and everyone else would probably lose several people and other important resources.

During the meeting he focused on what was happening. He heard someone say that the bankers had recommended eliminating the expensive Research and Development area for at least a year. That could save a lot of money quickly. Many of the people at the meeting thought the recommendation made sense.

However, one woman spoke up and said that they were not addressing the real problem. She said exactly what the young man had been thinking.

The young man spoke up, "Perhaps our real problem is that our current products are not as good as our competitors'. If we cut expenses in R&D we may save money now. But, if we don't invest in ourselves and develop good new products for The Future, the company itself could be in danger of going out of business in a few years."

His comments stimulated a strong discussion among the group.

Later in the week, with the support of his boss, the young man made a report on what customers wanted from their new products.

As he began to describe possible new products, he painted a picture of what the company's wonderful future might look like.

Over the next few months, several people took actions needed to develop the products customers wanted.

While not all of the new products lived up to expectations, one became a huge success, and once again the company flourished.

The young man was grateful he had learned to plan for The Future. Both he and his organization benefited from it.

OVER the years, the young man grew into a man.

He stayed in touch with the old man, who enjoyed knowing that the man was happy and successful.

However, one day the inevitable happened.

The old man died.

His wise voice could no longer be heard.

The man was stunned. He did not know how to respond.

The funeral that followed was attended by the city's leading men and women, as well as by boys and girls from the clubs the old man had sponsored.

Many rose to tell a wonderful story about the old man. It seemed he had helped many people.

As the man sat and listened, he realized how extraordinary the old man was. He had made such a difference in so many people's lives.

The man wondered, "What could I do to be like the old man, and help others?"

SEARCHING for answers, the man went back to the neighborhood where he had spent so many happy moments as a boy.

Years before, his parents had moved away, and the only times he had returned had been to visit the old man.

The old man's house was empty now, a "For Sale" sign planted in the lawn. He eyed the front porch swing where the old man had enjoyed spending his evenings.

He walked up on the porch and sat down gingerly on the swing, afraid the old chains might snap. As he settled back against the worn, wooden slats, the only sound he could hear was the creaking of the swing.

He thought over all that he had learned from the old man.

He knew he was now able to stay in The Present more often, focusing on what was right now, and paying attention to what was important. And he found it extraordinarily helpful.

Whenever he concentrated entirely on what he was doing, he was happier and he certainly did a better job.

He used what he learned from The Past to improve The Present. He had not repeated as many previous mistakes.

He had discovered that planning for The Future could often make The Future better. But he still felt that he needed to put it all in perspective, especially now that he no longer had the old man to rely on.

The man closed his eyes and gently swung back and forth on the swing, focusing only on The Present. He felt peaceful.

Gradually, he began to sense the old man sitting next to him on the porch. It was as if he were there.

He could almost hear the old man's voice replaying their many conversations. Once again, he experienced the wisdom of the old man's words, and felt the warmth of the old man's compassion.

He wondered why the old man had spent so much time helping him and others to learn about The Present.

The old man had many demands on his time. Why had he chosen to spend it on sharing The Present with others, rather than on more self-serving pursuits?

The man continued swinging back and forth, eyes closed, now focusing his energy only on this question. Slowly, gradually, the answer began to emerge.

The old man did these things because he had a Purpose that extended beyond self-gain. His Purpose – his reason for getting up in the morning – was to help others become happy and successful.

In fact, everything the old man did carried with it a sense of Purpose. Whether it was teaching about The Present, leading a company meeting, or spending leisure time with his family, the old man always acted with Purpose.

And, it was this sense of Purpose that tied The Present, Past, and Future together ... and gave his life meaning.

The man opened his eyes. This was it! This was the thread that pulled it all together.

The man reached for his notepad. He wrote:

Living in The Present, learning from The Past, and planning for The Future is not all there is.

It is only when you Live with Purpose and respond to what's important about The Present, Past and Future, that it all has meaning.

The man stopped and looked at the words he had just written. He thought about what they meant.

He understood that Living with Purpose means not just knowing *what* to do, but *why.*

Working and living with purpose is not some grand scheme or life plan. It is a practical approach for everyday life.

It means rising each day and seeing what meaning it will hold for you and others as a result of your actions.

He realized:

How You Respond
Depends Upon Your Purpose.

When You Want To Be Happy
And More Successful
It Is Time To Be
In The Present Moment.

When You Want The Present
To Be Better Than The Past
It Is Time To Learn From The Past.

When You Want The Future
To Be Better Than The Present
It Is Time To Plan For The Future.

*When You Live And
Work With Purpose,*

*And Respond To
What Is Important Now,*

*You Are More Able To
Lead, Manage, Support,
Befriend, And Love.*

The man now realized he needed to plan his future without his trusted mentor to guide him.

The man wondered if he knew enough.

Then he smiled. He knew what the old man would say:

The man knew enough. He had enough. He was enough.

Some people choose to receive The Present when they are young. Others when they are in middle age. Some when they are very old. And, some people never do.

As the man swung on the swing, he chose to return to The Present now.

He had found his Purpose. He would help others discover what he had learned!

He felt happy and successful.

Reflecting on what success was, he knew it meant various things to different people.

Success might be having a more peaceful life; doing a better job; enjoying quality time with family and friends; getting a promotion; being physically fit; making more money; or simply being a decent human who helps others.

With what the old man had taught him, and what he had discovered through his own experiences, he realized:

*Success Is Becoming Who You
Are Capable Of Being.*

*And Progressing Toward
Worthwhile Goals.*

*Each Of Us Defines For Ourselves
What It Means
To Be Successful.*

The man realized that he had learned to use the tools that can make anyone happy and successful.

It was so simple, he thought. The Present nourished him, aided by the lessons he had learned from The Past, and the planned goals he had set for The Future.

And by responding to what he experienced in The Present, he became more successful.

He focused on what was important. He was able to see and deal with opportunities and challenges as they came along. And he was able to appreciate his colleagues, family and friends.

He also realized that, because he was only human, he would not always be able to stay in The Present. He might lose it from time to time. But when that happened, he could always remind himself to return to The Present.

The Present would always be there for him. He could give himself the gift whenever he chose.

The man decided to write down a summary of what he had learned.

He would keep it before him on his desk, where he could be reminded of it daily.

The Present

THREE WAYS TO USE YOUR PRESENT MOMENTS

BE IN THE PRESENT
WHEN YOU WANT TO BE HAPPY AND SUCCESSFUL
Focus On What Is Right Now.
Use Your Purpose To Respond
To What Is Important Now.

LEARN FROM THE PAST
WHEN YOU WANT TO MAKE THE PRESENT BETTER THAN THE PAST
Look At What Happened In The Past.
Learn Something Valuable From It.
Do Things Differently In The Present.

PLAN FOR THE FUTURE
WHEN YOU WANT TO MAKE THE FUTURE BETTER THAN THE PRESENT
See What A Wonderful Future Would Look Like.
Make Plans To Help It Happen.
Put Your Plan Into Action In The Present.

IN the years that followed, the man used what he had learned over and over again.

He made adjustments along the way, depending on the situations he faced. He became better and better at what he did.

He received many promotions.

Eventually he became the head of his company, a man respected and admired by those who knew him.

Being with him made the people around him feel more alive. In his presence, they felt better about themselves.

He seemed to listen better than most people, to anticipate and solve problems, and see solutions before anyone else.

In his personal life, he had created a loving family. His wife and children cared about him as much as he cared for them.

In so many ways, he had become like the old man he so admired.

The man enjoyed sharing what he had discovered about The Present with others.

He knew that many people appreciated the story and learned from it, while others did not.

He realized, of course, that was up to them.

One morning, a group of new employees gathered in the man's office. He had a tradition of greeting all new employees personally.

A young woman noticed the framed card entitled "The Present" and said, "May I ask why you keep that on your desk?"

"Certainly," he responded.

"What's on the card is the summary of an inspiring and practical story I heard from a great man. It's about how to be happy and successful – in the broadest sense of those words.

"I find it's a real help to me."

Several people in the group looked over at the card.

"May I see it?" the woman asked.

"Of course."

The man handed her the framed card.

The young woman read it slowly, and then passed it to the others.

After she read the card, the young woman said, "This seems like it could be very helpful in a situation I am dealing with right now."

As she handed the framed card back to him, she said, "Can we hear the story?"

The group gathered around the conference table, and the man shared the story of The Present. Then he handed out several copies of the card he kept in his desk. "I hope it will help you as much as it has me."

Over the next few months, the man noticed that some of the new employees seemed to embrace The Present. Those who did thrived. Others were skeptical, or simply put it aside.

Sometime later, the young woman who asked about The Present, re-entered his office.

She had taken on more responsibility and seemed to excel at her job. "I just want to thank you for the story of The Present," she said. "I keep the card with me and refer to it often. It's been invaluable."

Then she left the man's office.

Over time, the woman shared the story with family, friends and business colleagues.

Many of the people who heard the story prospered, and so did their organizations.

And the man was pleased to see that what he had learned from the old man was helping the next generation.

SEVERAL decades later, the man, now happy, prosperous and respected, had become an old man himself.

His children had grown and had families of their own. His wife had become his best friend and closest companion.

Although he had retired from business, The Present continued to provide him with abundant energy, and he and his wife devoted themselves generously to other pursuits in the community.

One day, a young couple with a little girl moved in down the street. Before long, the family came by to visit.

The little girl enjoyed listening to "the old man," as she came to call him. It was fun to be with him. There was something special about him, although she didn't know what it was. He seemed happy, and he made her feel happy and good about herself.

"What makes him so special?" she wondered. "How could someone so old, be so happy?"

One day she asked him. The old man smiled. And he told her about The Present.

The little girl jumped up with delight.

As she ran off to play, the old man heard her exclaim, "Wow!

"I hope someday someone gives me …

The Present!

After The Story

After The Story

As Bill finished the story, Liz smiled and said, "I needed that."

She added, "As you probably noticed, I have been taking many notes. Obviously, there's a lot to think about."

She was quiet for a few moments, as she reflected on what she had just heard.

Finally she said, "Thanks very much for sharing the story, Bill."

Then she said, "I think I'm going to try to put it to use, and see what happens for myself. After I do, can we talk again?"

Bill agreed, "Of course."

"It was great to see you," Liz said. And, after a moment or two of pleasantries, she was gone.

As she left, Bill wondered what his friend had gained from the story.

He would have to wait a while to find out.

Then, one morning at work, after his weekly team meeting, Bill found a message on his voice mail. It was from Liz.

"Bill, are you free for lunch anytime soon?"

Several days later, when Bill arrived at the restaurant, Liz was already there. She didn't look tired or anxious – just the opposite. He said, "You look great, Liz. What's up?"

She smiled. "You remember that story you told me, The Present?"

He nodded. "Of course I remember."

"Well, many things have happened since, and I couldn't wait another moment to tell you about them.

"After our lunch meeting, I saw you had changed so much since we worked together – and for the better!

"So I started to think more about the story because it had obviously worked for you.

"A few days later at work, it came back to me again.

"I was getting stressed out with my boss. I was over-worked and tired, and she was pushing us to make changes in our marketing plan. Changes I didn't think were necessary. And given everything else we had to do, I'm afraid I resented her for asking us to do more.

"She kept talking about how the economy and marketplace were changing and how we needed to adapt. But I didn't want to hear it.

"It was the same old speech she's made before. She said a new marketing plan was long overdue. But this time, she said that I was still riding on my old successes. That I was holding onto The Past.

"My first reaction was to block out what she was saying, knowing how many other projects I had to do.

"But I recalled the part in the story where the old man said, '*You can learn from The Past but it is not wise to be in The Past.*' I began to wonder if that was where I have been for too long – in The Past.

"And I worried a lot about The Future, too – I felt unprepared for it."

She laughed and said, "I guess I've been spending time almost everywhere except in The Present!

"Anyway, I thought about the story, especially the part at the end."

"What part?" Bill asked.

"Where the man realized that being in The Present meant being aware of what your Purpose is right now, and *responding* to it."

"I didn't quite understand it at first. But I found myself every once in a while stopping and asking, 'What is my Purpose right now? And what am I doing to make it a reality?' "

"That's when I went back and reviewed my notes which I re-wrote so they were more understandable. And I added some ways I could put what I learned to use. Then I tried it.

"The first time was at home one morning when I was getting ready for work. All too often, I've been 'too busy' during breakfast when my son wanted my attention.

"But, when I focused on The Present, and realized my Purpose, I was able to give my son all the attention he needed – to be truly present with him. I listened to what was important to him, right at that moment. It made both my son and me happy. Now we enjoy such times more often.

"It's amazing how little effort it takes to be fully in The Present, and what a big difference it makes."

Liz said, "I'm surprised by the effect the story is having, not just on me, but also on others I have told it to."

"Others?" Bill asked.

"Well, for example, one day, one of our star sales people looked like he was feeling down. So I suggested we have coffee together.

"When I asked what was bothering him, he complained that his commission pay was barely half what it was at this time last year. I asked him why, and he said something like, 'The market is terrible right now. No one could make sales in this kind of environment.'

"Then he started getting really worked up. He told me, 'My boss thinks the reason I can't bring in the sales the way I used to is because I'm slacking off. I couldn't believe it. I made this company a lot of money last year. Shouldn't that count for something?' "

Liz said, "So I told him the story of The Present. Well, that was more than three weeks ago. Then, just the other day, he stopped by my desk with a big grin on his face. I asked, 'What are you smiling about?'

" 'I just landed a huge sale!' he exclaimed. We talked for a while. He said he was doing better because he had learned how to let go of The Past and live more in The Present.

"He said when he'd thought about how much more money he used to make and how little he made now, it angered him and his customers sensed it.

" 'Now whenever I see a negative look on my customer's face,' he said, 'I make a mental note of what I am thinking about – usually about how hard it is to make a sale this year compared to last year.

" 'Then I ask myself what my Purpose is right now and am I responding to making my sales quota, or serving my customer's needs?

" 'More often than not, I wake up and realize that my own worries and concerns are not what's important to them. I realize my Purpose is to help my customers get what they need.

" 'When I let go of The Past, and fully engage in The Present, I focus on how I can help my customers meet their needs, right now – and nothing else. And when I do that – voila! – the sales come.' "

Liz went on, "He's discovered that he should just do the best job he can '*today*.' As that is all he really has control over.

"He says it's amazing how much it helps him.

"And, he said that as soon as he figured it out, the stress began to lift. The next thing he knew, he was enjoying his work again.

"He actually wrote out several quotes from the story – at least the way he remembered them – and posted them on his office wall! I've seen them!"

Bill looked at his friend and smiled. "That's terrific," he said. "Did you tell anyone else about The Present?"

"As a matter of fact, I did!" Liz continued.

"My best friend at work went through an awful divorce a while ago. It left her hurt and angry, and it was affecting her work. She was late with a couple of projects, and when she called in sick one too many times, her boss became annoyed with her.

"That evening, I went to her house. We talked for quite a while. Eventually I told her the story of The Present.

"A few days later my friend put a bowl on my desk. She told me that every time she was not in The Present, and started to think about her divorce and how angry she was at her ex-husband, she would come to my office and put a dollar in the bowl.

"She said if she ever stopped putting dollars in, we would go to dinner on her. She laughed; she was sure there would be enough money to pay for an expensive meal.

"The first few weeks, she'd come in every hour or so and she'd throw in a dollar or two, or three for each time she had allowed herself to dwell on what might have been, or what should have been. But slowly, the number of dollars fell. And this week, incredibly, the bowl has not collected a single dollar.

"She told me the other day it was only when she could physically see how much time and money she was wasting by mulling over the past, that she understood how much harm she was doing to herself.

"She couldn't concentrate at work, her friends were fed up with her complaints, and her energy had bottomed out.

"She was acting as though her purpose was to remain hurt and angry, versus moving on and improving her life.

"She says the more she lets go of The Past, the more she can focus now on The Present.

"She says what she finds especially helpful is picturing what a wonderful future would look like.

"Now, when she drives home from work, she plans how she wants to be with her children when she gets home.

"A moment before she gets out of her car and steps into her house, she imagines how she wants to be with her family over the next few hours. She sees herself not getting distracted by the newspaper or the television.

"She sees herself more as a relaxed person, enjoying her house and being a loving parent.

"She's amazed how much better things are going at home now.

"Needless to say," Liz said, "my friend is now doing a much better job at work as well. Several people have noticed it, especially her boss.

"She came into my office this morning, saying, 'Looks like next week we are going to enjoy a great dinner – on me!' "

Bill said, "That's wonderful, Liz."

"It *is,* isn't it!" Liz responded.

Then she added, "I told my husband about how much better my co-workers and I were doing at work and how much of it was due to using what we'd learned from The Present.

"My husband," she went on, "is always worried about how we are going to pay for things, like the twins' college tuition, even though they are only five years old.

"He obsesses over getting promoted and making more money so we can buy a bigger house. He's afraid we won't have enough money to retire later.

"I love him for feeling responsible and caring about our family. But I see the stress it puts on him even if he doesn't realize it.

"I had wanted to tell him the story of The Present but was determined not to do so until he wanted to hear it.

"One evening he asked me about it. So, I poured him a glass of his favorite wine, and told him the story.

"I wasn't sure he was paying attention. But when I'd finished, he said, 'What I like about the story is how you worry less when you have a plan for The Future. Because The Future becomes more known to you.'

"He asked, 'What was it the old man said in The Present? *It is important to plan for The Future if you want The Future to be better than The Present.*'

"Then he added, 'I don't think you and I do that often enough.'"

Liz went on, "And he was right. I didn't plan enough for The Future either. It's been a big shortcoming.

"My husband suggested, 'Let's carve out time on Saturday morning to go over our finances.'

"I agreed and said, 'In the meantime we can pull together our financial records and anything else you think we need.' He seemed happy about that.

"We had a very good financial planning session, the best we've ever had. We dealt with a number of things that we had been putting off.

"Later that week, my husband came up to me and gave me a big hug. I asked him why he was in such a good mood and he said, 'I feel so much better.'

"Why?" I asked.

"He said, 'In thinking about that story, I realized that I've been so preoccupied with our future that I haven't been able to enjoy what we have right now – *today!*

" 'I've been breaking my back to make more and more money. And suddenly I realized even if I make a million dollars a year, there will always be something that we can't afford or prepare for.'

"He came to realize he was working too hard on his 'business future' and not enjoying his 'family present.' He had forgotten *why* he was working so hard in the first place.

"He said he was acting as if making money was his Purpose, versus loving and supporting our family through the money he made.

"He said, 'I understand that I need to take each day more as it comes, and live it thoroughly, rather than second guessing The Future. As long as the kids see that you and I are happy together, they're going to be happy no matter what kind of house we live in or what kind of car we drive.

" 'While it's important that we plan for The Future, like we did last weekend, we shouldn't *live* in The Future. I see the difference now.' "

Liz was quiet for a moment, recalling the experience with her husband.

Bill smiled. Then he asked, "Are you successful in applying this same kind of thinking at work?"

"Yes," Liz answered. "We got a report recently that one of our divisions was losing sales on what had been one of our most popular products.

"There were rumors that there would be budget cuts and layoffs, not unlike what happened in the story.

"It made many of us anxious because some of our friends might lose their jobs. I asked myself what I could do about it. I realized that we needed to focus on developing newer and better products.

"I sent out a memo asking everyone to think about the future of our products and scheduled a two hour meeting for the next morning.

"The meeting was so full of energy, it lasted an hour longer than I expected. But, by lunch we had made a major breakthrough.

"Later that afternoon, people came back with several worthwhile refinements.

"I found that by planning for The Future, we had begun to achieve what we needed to do. And then I was able to refocus and act on The Present needs of the company.

"At the end of the day, I went to my daughter's summer league soccer game. And, while I was there, I focused on The Present, on her, putting aside thoughts about our future products. I could get to that tomorrow.

"And when the game was over, I was able to be there for her, in The Present, in a way I never had been before.

"I realize, of course, that what's important right *now* is always changing. But my overall Purpose gives me clearer direction in everything I do.

"I find that if I focus on what's at hand at the present moment, I do so much better.

"And I'm not the only one. So many people at work and in my family have learned to do this as well."

Bill asked, "Did you share your notes with them?"

"As a matter of fact, I did!" Liz answered. "I expanded on my notes and wrote down the story as well as I could remember it. Then I shared it with several people.

"I'll admit that not everyone who has heard or read the story has benefited from it. There are more than a few people at work who don't get it.

"But the people who do get it have made a positive impact on our company," she continued. "It's actually made quite a big difference!"

Liz suggested, "Maybe you would like to come over and see for yourself."

Bill said he would love to, and would arrange to do so soon.

Then Liz looked at her watch and realized that she needed to get back. She picked up the check and said, "I really want to thank you, Bill, for introducing me to the story of The Present. It has changed everything."

"You're welcome, Liz," Bill said. "I'm glad you put the story to such good use.

"And it's good to see you recognize that the more people live and work in The Present, the more they, and their families, and organizations benefit. As you have found out for yourself."

"Well," Liz said, "I found it to be a wonderful blueprint to use whether I'm working on a project, or just spending quality time with my family."

She said, "It's a great source of inspiration and practical guidance.

"I'm definitely going to use it more in our organization. When you find something that works, you want to have as many people use it as soon as you can."

She added, "When people are happy and successful – at work and at home, it's better for everybody."

Bill smiled and said, "What happened to my friend 'the skeptic'?"

Liz smiled back at him and said, "Maybe she just gave herself ...

THE PRESENT!!!

the end

To Learn More ...

*To learn more about products and services
for individuals and organizations
based on The Present, visit:*

www.ThePresent.com

or call: 1-800-851-9311

TWO EDITIONS OF THIS STORY

Spencer Johnson's classic book *The Precious Present* was first published by Doubleday in 1984. The simple, charming story focuses on a single idea that has helped, and continues to help, many people appreciate what they have and who they are.

Now, Bantam is proud to publish this new book of Dr. Johnson's, *The Present*, which builds on the original idea in *The Precious Present*. As you may have discovered, this powerful story of inspiration and practical guidance reveals profound insights that can bring you a sense of fulfillment and success in business and in life.

Each book reveals its own timeless truths, and we are delighted that both versions are now available.

BANTAM BOOKS

About The Author

Spencer Johnson, M.D., is one of the most respected and beloved authors in the world. He has helped tens of millions of people discover how they can enjoy better lives by using simple truths that lead to fulfillment and success at work and at home.

Inspiring and entertaining people with his insightful stories that speak directly to the heart and soul, he is often referred to as the best there is at taking complex subjects and presenting simple solutions that work.

Dr. Johnson is the author or co-author of numerous *New York Times* bestselling books, including the #1 Bestsellers *Who Moved My Cheese? — An A-Mazing Way to Deal with Change In Your Work and In Your Life*, and *The One Minute Manager®*, the world's most popular management method, co-authored with Kenneth Blanchard.

After graduating with a B.A. in psychology from the University of Southern California, Dr. Johnson received his M.D. degree from the Royal College of Surgeons, and completed medical clerkships at the Mayo Clinic and the Harvard Medical School.

He served as Director of Communications for Medtronic, the inventors of cardiac pacemakers; Research Physician at The Institute for Inter-Disciplinary Studies; Consultant to The Center for Study of the Person; and more recently as Leadership Fellow at the Harvard Business School.

His work has captured the attention of major media, including CNN, the *Today* show, *Time,* the BBC, *Business Week, New York Times, Reader's Digest, Wall Street Journal, Fortune, USA Today*, Associated Press and United Press International.

His books are available in forty languages.